LEARNING SOCIAL BEHAVIORAL ECONOMIC PSYCHOLOGY

JOHN LOK

Contents

PREFACE

Introduction

Behavioral economy is one useful and fun social subject. Behavioral economists usually research how and why human behaviors may

influence economy growth or recession, or how and why economy environment changing factor may influence human behavior changes.

Nowadays, many businessmen or marketing research professional hope to apply different methods to predict consumer behaviors in order to know what will be future market activities and market changes to help them to choose to implement what kinds of marketing strategies more accurately.

The methods include economic environmental change prediction method, consumer individual psychological change prediction method, micro or macro behavioral economic environmental change prediction method, marketing environmental change prediction method etc. different kinds of methods which can be applied to predict how consumer behavioral changes to influence whose behavioral consumption to the manufacturer products sale within one to two years short term or three to five years middle term, even above five years long term business plans. What factors may influence passengers choose to catch underground train in preference? What factors may influence students to choose to learn from distance learning in preference? What factors may influence traveler individual overseas travelling times?

In my this book final part, I shall considerate on businessmen and customers both beneficial view point to explain how to apply behavioral economic concept to predict how their specific industries marketing development trend or consumer behavioral changing trend in these micro economic (individual consumer psychological shopping change trend) and macro-economic (global every specific industry marketing changing trend) environment.

In my this book, I shall attempt to explain how and why ecommerce may be one kind network human job. Also, I shall indicate reasons to explain why human network behavior may bring direct or indirect influences to economy growth or recession in our global societies in macro and micro economy view. I shall indicate cases to explain any possible human social activities may bring direct or indirect influences to cause our social economic growth or recession in consequence in possible. I hope that my readers can feel more understanding whether what real meaning of behavioral economy is the relationship between our behaviors and our economy.

PROLOGUE

Contents

How can airline atmosphere environment influence traveler travel choice behavior?

How can airline counter servicer knowledge influence traveler consumption behavior?

In -store consumer digital signage behavior how can influence consumer behavior

Chapter 6

Influence passenger catching underground train psychology factor

How does MTR (Mass Train Railway) need to

consider route design location of choice by (AI)

marketing research survey method? p.67-77

Why MTR underground train transportation needs to know passenger behavior 78-79

Why route choice can influence passenger behavioral choice

Why trip time reliability and crowding factors can influence MTR passenger choice.

How to apply online psychological advertising method to predict passenger behavioral consumption?

Does habit strength moderate the intention behavior to consumption?

I

Human Behavioral network job brings social economic benefits

What does human network job mean ? Why may human network job be popular? Why human network job behavior may influence economy ?

Nowadays internet is popular to use. We can apply internet to find data , search any new things, even earn money. Why does internet

may become huma network job source. For example, e-publish may be one kind of new human network job. Any authors may apply internet

channel to help them to sell electronic or paper books from e-publisher web store. They may apply facebook, you tub etc. any online

channel to promote themselves new books to let new readers to know whether when they may buy themselves favourable new topic books to read

from electronic publisher web store.

Thus, future electronic publisher industry may help any authors to build internet network platform to help them to sell and promote

to advertise their any one new electronic or paper book topic to let global any one reader to choose to buy their any new topic books from electronic publisher web store easily and conveniently. However, it implies that electronic network platform author may be one kind of future new human network job in our societies.

How electronic network platform author job may bring economy benefit in macro economy view? A person can have few friends, contacts and still be very influential if these few

friends and contacts are themselves highly influential, e.g. one author must not need to know any one reader in global society. When they like to choose any electronic books from electronic internet network platform. They may become the author's any one topic book buyer, when they feel the author's any one topic book is fun and attract they make decision to both the strange author whose the topic book from electronic book publisher's platform web store convenience in short time. Although, they are strangers, they do not know themselves , but the reader can understand what it way that made Google from writing platform to create new creative mind and typing network job method to replace traditional hand writing book method for global authors. It will be one kind of new human network writing job.

Hence, global any one reader can apply an innovative search engine , such as google.com to find whether whom author personal new topic books are value to read from internet.

Then, the electroniuc publisher's web store may be new book store platform sale network to help the author to sell many electronic or paper books from electronic network platform

in short time. So, internet may be future new network plaform to help global any one author to create network writing job absolutely. Furthermore, internet may be popular social media

to help any one author to build goold relationship between his/her readers. It is one kind of new network, human network job. New authors do not need to buy many paper books to prepare to put in any one book shop warehouse. Their every book can print on demand to reduce out of book stock in any one book shop. They may choose to sell either electronic books or paper books both from any one book publisher web store. So, electronic network platform may be one kind of good writing channel to help human authors to create income and it can also

help authors to bring new creative mind and new topic fun content books to let readers to know and buy to read from electronic publisher network platform.

Why does human behavior may be one kind of new human network job to bring global economic advantages. ALthough, it may be free income or without inocme, but the person does the network behavior, his/her behavior may be bring advantages to influence many other people's health. For this case, when a worker in a coffee shop in an airport gets a vaccination aganinst the flu, it does not only helps him or her stay healthy, but also helps the many travellers who might otherwise have been inflected if that workers caught the flu.

So, the externality , the result implies the vaccination of even a part of a community conveys benefits to the whole community. For example, governments pay special attention

to the vaccinations of school children, teachers, health mothers, and the elderly, categories of people particularly susceptible not only to catching, but also to transmitting a disease.

It is not accidential that governments are heavily involved with vaccination . When there are externalities, free market, fail to persuade individual incentives with society's

their the worker's decision of whether to get a vaccine ends up attracting whether other people get sick. The workers might not

fully take all these other people's potential suffering into account when making her or his vaccination decision.

As Stanford University does many suggestions, understand this and tries to help them make the right decisions and so providers free flu vaccines for its staff and students.

Small pockets of unvaccinated individuals can allow a disease to gain a spread more widely well-being. For example, parent weighing the costs and benefits of a vaccine for their child is not always thinking of the consequences of that vaccination to other people. THese are markets in which subsidizing or regulating behavior can make everyone better off. Because the reason for requiring that a child be vaccinated before enrolling in school is not just to protect that child, because each child's vaccination affects others via potential contagions.

II

Robots take our jobs behavioral and economy influences

Robot job behavior brings economy influences

If one day robots can replace human to do simple, even complex jobs. They will bring what influences to our global social economy.The popular economic refrain declares that the

global middle class is dying and robots will soon take our jobs, e.g. shopping center customer service jobs, library service jobs, cinema ticket sale jobs, restaurant kitchen cooker jobs,

even, bus drivers, taxi drivers etc. public transport driving jobs, accountant, doctors etc. professional jobs. Whether it is beautiful or petty matter if our future societies have many human jobs can be replaced to do from robots. Businessman must may reduce to employ employees and reduce to pay salary or wage, when robots can be replaced to do their employees tasks. But, societies must bring un-employment rate rises , due to societies will have many people loss jobs when their employers choose to buy robots to serve their clients or do any office tasks or customer service or cleaning etc. tasks.

In micro economy view, employers may save money in long term, but in macro economy view, it will cause unemployment ratio rises , even crime rate rises when there are many people lose jobs in societies. These models of doom, though, fail to account for the hundreds of businesses riding the waves of change in their industries when robots may be invented to replace human to do many simple , even complex tasks in our future societies.

WE may image that one small factory needs to manufacture fishes canes to sell to supermarket, the small , cheaper stuff and higher margin parts of the fishes manufacture industry. Before, this factory needs to employ many human factory workers need to help every fresh customer making the perfect fishing gear, designed for performance, durability, and cost in order to achieve to manufacture every fish cane in whole fished processing manufacturing stages. Every worker needs to spend about 15 to twenty minutes to finish every fish cane , till to delivery to any supermarket to sell. If this fish canes manufacturing factory can apply manufacturing robots to help them to finish any one working tasks , every robot can only spend five minutes to finish whole fresh fish cane manufacturing process. Thus, every robot can help this factory save 10 to 15 minutes time to fish every fish cane manufacturing process. IN fact, time is money, because when every robot can help this factory to reduce 10 to 15 minutes time to compare human worker. Then, this factory can finish about 20 fish canes in one hour if it can use robot to help it to manufacture fish canes. Otherwise, if this factory still use human workers to help it to manufacture fish canes, then it can fish about 3 to 4 fish canes in one hour. SO, the manufacturing efficiency ensures that robots must help this fish manufacturing factory to raise fish canes number more than human workers. So, in robotic behavioral economy view, manufacturing robots must help this fish canes manufacturing factory to raise fish canes manufacturing number and deliver increasing number to supermarkets to prepare to sell every day. Robots can help this fish canes manufacturing factory bring manufacturing time saving, rising manufacturing efficiency, improving performance and reducing wages expenditure long time advantages in micro economy view. However, manufacturing robots can also bring disadvanages to society, e.g. increasing unemployment ratio, increasing crime rate,

this factory workers will lose jobs and income, they need earn social welfare from government and increasing government finance pressure in short time, even long time in macro economic view.

Stanford University graduate program in economics, Scott lecturer explained that "in demand and supply economic theory for robots supply and demand case, robots supply number increasing may influence human workers demand number decrease. It sometimes calls " the efficient frontier".

No specific human beings were mentioned in any of economics classes. As robots supply and demand in market case, They (robots) may be purely theoretical " agents" who reached to the most reasonable sale prices in order to persuade any one businessman buyer to make manufacturing robot buying decision whether robots can help him / her to bring how much saving time , saving money, saving cost, improving performance, efficiency economic benefit before he/she plans to reduce workers number when he/ she decides to apply robots to replace human workers in his/her factory or office or any service department, e.g. cinema ticket sale service, shopping center customer service, shopping center cleaning , supermarket customer service etc. service or sale tasks. When robots can replace human to do any one of these tasks in any organizations. So, robots may be human worker agents who reached to prices the way robots would react to a software

command. There was nothing that explained why some people thrived and others did n't or why truly brilliant, hardworking people could fail when much lazier folks succeeded." Having been admitted to the Stanford University graduate program in economics, Scott lecturer hoped to get his answers there.

How robots influence our future social changing? Using the right technology can be a boon to your business in this economy. For internet example, it is easier than ever to find well-matched customers

all around the world, to stay in contact with them, and to more quickly design the products they want. If you focus solely on being cutting -edge, though you risk letting the technology

take over what should be very robust relationships with your customers , employees, and colleagues. IN nowaddays society, technoligical advances and cutomation, personal

relationships in business are more crucial than ever. I mean that robots can not replace human to serve clients to let them to feel more comfortable and passion more easily. For shoe shop case example, if the shoe shop apply one robot to serve its clients to replace human shoe salesperson to serve its shoe customers. Robots ensure that they can not persuade every shoe potential buyer to make shoe buying decision more easily when robots need to contact every shoe potential buyer. The reason is simple, because robots can not touch any one shoe buyer individual emotion very easier.

If the shoe buyer needs the robots to help him/her to choose any right shoe styles when he/she can not feel himself / herself can make the most right shoe style choice decision. The robots can not replace human shoe salesperson to make shoe style choice judgement more easily. They must need longer time to analyze whether which shoe style may be the most suitable to the shoe buyer. Otherwise,human shoe salesperson may attempt to make the most right shoe style choice decision to help any one shoe buyer to chooce the most right style shoe because he/she owns shoe style sale experience, shoe style knowledge, the most important reason is that they can feel every shoe customer individual emotion to touch whether he/she will feel comfortable or happy when they attempt to help every shoe customer to seek the most right shoe style in every shoe customer whole shoe searching processing. Othwerwise, serving robots are only one machine, they can not touch or feel every shoe customer individual emotion whether he/she feel comfortable or unhappy or happy when they need to contact them in whole shoe searching processing. Hence, I believe that some tasks robots can not repalce human staff to do very easily. Otherwise, robots may bring disadvanatges to let any one businessman to loss his/her customers, due to robots can not touch every customer

emotion to compare human staff in service tasks more easily. Robots serving customer behaviors may cause money lose and customers number lose to the shop in micro economic view.

III

Intellectual human economic behaviors

What does intellectual human economic behaviors mean ? I believe that when we choose or decide to do intellectual behaviors, then our societies will be influenced to bring economic growth in consequence.I shall attempt to indicate pollution case to explain how and why eithet our intellectual or foolish behaviors may bring economic growth or recession in consequence as below:

On one hand, for air pollution social case aspect example, if we only consider to buy cars to drive for working aim or holiday leisure aim. Then, our societies air will be polluted. Our health will be influenced to bad. Our car driving behaviors may cause global environment air pollution seriously. In long time, global air pollution will bring our bodies health to be bad. Although, ourselves car driving behaviors may bring our driving travelling leisure enjoyment and comfortable feeling in short time, also we so not need to pay public transport fare often, but we need to compensate ourselves health economic intangible loss due to air pollution , when cars number increases, dirty air will cause ourselves health to become bad.

In the result, we will need to pay more medical expenditure when we are old age, due to ourselves bodies will become bad, due to we breathe global dirty air every day, due to ourselves cars pollute air in long time, e.g. 10 to 20 years, even 30 more without limited air pollution environment. So, driving cars behavior may be one kind of human foolish behavior and our foolish behavior may bring ourselves future long time medical expenditure absolutely.

One the other hand, water pollution social aspect, if we often keep much rubbish to pollute sea, oil exploration processing pollute ocean , ships gas pollute ocean, then fishes will eat polluted food and drive dirty water, due to global ocean is polluted.

In fact, because human only to consider how to buy boats to carry on leisure enjoyment activities, or catch cruises to travel on the sea. Also, oil manufacturers only consider researching anywhere to find new oil exploration places to manufacture oil product, when their oil exploration processes pollute ocean . Consequently, global fishes drink polluted water or eat polluted food. They will have poison. SO, human will have high chance to eat poison polluted fishes, due to fishes are poison or are polluted.

So, human is doing foolish activities, we only hope to find oil exploration places to pollute ocean or we only spend money to buy ticket to catch ships to travel anywhere in global ocean. All of these human foolish behaviors will bring pollution to global ocean. On consequently, we will need to compensate to eat polluted or dirty or poison fishes, ourselves bodies health will be bad. In long time, we need have high chance to pay medical expenditure when we are old. So, pollution case may be one good example to explain how and why human foolish behavior may influence ourselves future need to compensate serious medical loss.

All of these human foolish behavior will bring pollution to global ocean. On consequently, we will need to compensate to eat polluted or dirty or poison fished , ourselves bodies health will be bad. In long time, we will have high chance to pay medical expenditure, when we are old. So, pollution case may be one good example to explain how and why human ourselves intellectual or foolish behaviors may influence future long time economic loss or economic growth or recession in micro and micro economic view.

On another water pollution aspect hand, if we often keep rubbish to sea, oil exploration processing pollutes ocean and ships' gas pollute ocean, then fishes will eat polluted food and drink dirty water, due to fishes will eat polluted food and drink dirty sea water because the global ocean is polluted seriously.

In fact, because human only consider how to buy boats to carry on any leisure water activities, or catches cruises to travel on the sea. Also, oil manufacturers only consider any where to find oil exploration places to manufacture oil products from ocean, when their pol exploration processes can pollute ocean. Consequently, global fishes drink polluted water or eat dirty food. They will have poison. So, human will have high chance to eat poison fishes.

Otherwise, such as pollution case, it can influence inflation or deflation. Consequently, the reason indicates supply and demand theory. If air pollution is serious, then we will consider health issue, global cars demand number may be influenced to reduce, when global cars number demand will reduce, global car prices and supply number will need to change to fall down in order to attract or persuade global car consumers choose to make car purchase decision.

Hence, global car manufacture number and car price will be influenced to reduce, due to global air pollution issue. Consequently, deflation will occur because when the country citizen usually does not spend much extra saving money to buy car expensive goods. Money value will be low. Otherwise, if global car pollution is not serious, human considers to buy cars to enjoy driving leisure lives. So, global car demand is influenced to increase , also global car price will also influenced to increase.

Consequently, global human will choose to buy cars to drive. Due to we accept to spend extra saving to buy expensive car goods. Car sale price and supply may be influenced to rise up. Money value is influenced to reduce. Inflation may be influenced, due to global car consumers number increases, we would not have extra money to spend easily. Car expensive goods expenditure influences our spending habit to avoid to make car purchase decision more easily. So, human intellectual or foolish activities may bring inflation or deflation consequence in possible indirectly in macro economic view.

On conclusion, above pollution case explain that how and why human intellectual or foolish economic behaviors may bring inflation or deflation consequence as well as economic growth or recession consequence as well as any goods demand and supply increasing or decreasing consequence. It implies that human behavior may have indirect relationship to influence any goods demand and supply number to either increase or decrease result as well as any goods price will be influenced to increase or decrease in micro and macro economic view.

IV

University campus choice and teaching method choice student psychological economy factor

University campus location factor

University can attempt to predict student individual psychological needs to avoid student turnover numbers increasing and campus location factor can influence students‘ studying choices. Whether University location can be a competitive advantage to attract students to study? The school (university) location means that the proximity of city center and the proximity of students home. To increase the occupancy rate, the university location is needed to provide as a model and resources based view which will be used to explain why the school location is a kind of competitive advantage for universities. According to Porter theory, it is a part of factor, which has some advantages against the treat of entry. It can decrease the treatment of rivalry. However, a good place has a certainly positive effect for attracting staff and more students. For resource-based view, the location is one of the internal resources for long term economic benefit production of factor. It can be accepted as one of the physical and tangible resource of a university.

I shall apply the first attractive factor of Porter five forces and resource based model to analyze my opinion to explain why school (university location) can influence students to choose the university to study. This view is represented by the opportunities and the threats. The university of thought is the resource based view which is represented by the strengths and weaknesses of the firm. Porter's five force model of competition elements include threats of entrants or substitutes, bargaining power of buyers or suppliers and competition rivalry. A firm's resources include brand name, in-house knowledge of technology, employment of skilled personnel, trade contract, machinery, efficient procedures and capital etc. Such as, both tangible and intangible assets are considered a firm's resources. For a university, customers can be thought as a students, suppliers can be thought as staff. In higher education industry, the good transportation infrastructure and well-connected universities have some advantages against the treat of entry to attract good staff and more students. The place of a university can decrease of treatment of rival and a good place has certainty positive location is an opportunity for universities to attract the students.

The resource based theory of university location competitive advantage

Students choose any one university to study who will judge whether economic cost is reasonable to decide to study the school, e.g. school fee, transportation cost etc. According to the Porter's theory, the resource based theory can apply competitive resources to be identifies to higher education institutions. For higher education institutions, such as resources might include the reputation of certain departments, the grouping together of areas of specialist expertise and the development of technical patents etc. Also higher education resources may not be imperfectly mobile, as the competitive resources of a university identifies tangible, intangible and organizational assets. So, the tangible resources might include campus location, building capacity, conference facilities and medical research facilities. Intangible resources generally include such items as patents, teaching and research performance, service levels and technology and the geographical location of a service. In a university, such intangible resources might include some of the above and may also include employees/ associates, e.g. experienced professors, renowned authors and distinguished teachers. Also, the location of a university can be accepted as physical and tangible resources of a university. However, I believe location is shown as an important factor to affect the students' university enrolment selection decisions.

To sources of competitive advantages are thought to be the reputation of the institution, the curriculum and educational standards, school fees (tuition), location and student activities etc. different factors. Moreover, any university's general client segments include such as, high school graduates, elderly students and international students, that have been influenced by several factors when selecting the best university to study. One of these factors is again location, the proximity to home and easy transportation is critical factor in selecting a university. Presumably, institutions that are located along well-established public transit routes have a competitive advantage over those with poor transit links. Due to the efficiency of innovation activity increased in easily accessible locations with a high density of economic activity. The existence of education and research institutions as well as easily available information is suggested as a reason for this increase. Also private higher education institutions desire to benefit from these flows by locating itself nearby. Therefore, together with other factors, such as existing capital global flows should be existing capital and population, level of income and location decisions of foundation universities. The location, social life campus, proximity of campus to the city center, exchange programs, the curricula infrastructure, languages medium of instruction and activities are the most significant factors to influence students to choose which university to study. By the past statistic indicated that the location has 94% rate, the proximity of campus to the city center has 84% rate. So, it seems the proximity of campus to the city center factor is more prior choice to compare with the school location is close to the student home factor.

Huang (2012) stated that " the right location attracts more students and ensures the revenues of the institution. The location of an educational institution might influence its future prospect of growth. A good location attracts not only more students, but also excellent teaching staff". Because of job opportunities areas, the students are able to get a part-time job and earn extra money for their tuition (Huang, 2012). Marketing concept has four "P", it can apply to university educational business, such as educational promotion, tuition price, teachers of people and school campus location of place.

Finally, I shall give two assumptions to explain why if the university location is not popular to be accepted to the country's students in general, then it will cause who won't choose to study the university. However, even if the university's tuition is reasonable or cheaper or lecturers are famous or reputation or educational advertisement is attractive. In fact, the poor location factor will influence many local or overseas students who don't choose to study the university in the country. The first assumption is that most of students feel that the proximity of the university to the city center factor affects their university final choice decision and the another assumption is that most of students feel that the proximity of university to home affects their university final choice decision. There two assumptions are used to determine the importance of university location to attract the students. In Porter theory, either proximity of city center and/or proximity of student's home of a university factors have same advantages against the treat of entry. It can decrease the treatment of rival and a good place has certainly positive effect to attract teaching staff and more students. In resource based view, the location can be accepted a kind of internal resources. It can be accepted as one of the sustainable competitive advantages literature, location is a kind of advantage for higher education institutions.

The factor of student demand for alternative modes of course delivery is another factor to influence the student who chooses the university to study. Any university's educational program includes program design, material production (both print and e-version), promotion, essay competition, school networks, budgeting, coordinating with various constructors, data base management and program evaluation etc.

Nowadays, university teaching methods may include face-to face, online and hybrid modes of course delivery. However, the several ways to students to deliver their course works ,such as full time, part time, internal/ non campus, external studies/distance education, summer school, winter school, semester study and trimester study. The multi site of a university , e.g. major provider of distance online education operates popular affordable learning for student to use internet to study. Although, students do not need to attend to university classroom to listen lecturer's teaching, but it can reduce face-to-face contact between lecturers and students in university classroom often.

Although, it is a technological and innovative and effective learning modalities. In fact, such new technological teaching modalities may be necessitated to the graduated or master degree or doctoral degree students. But, I feel the online teaching method is not suitable to the bachelor degree students. As the delivery of course content or the commoditization of knowledge must be re-thought to the bachelor's if the student can't enquire whose lecturer any questions to give feedback by face-to-face. Then, who will concern the course to feel more difficult possibly if who can't listen whose lecturer's opinion to solve whose challenges about the course any questions immediately in classroom often.

The second attractive factor of student demand for alternative modes of course delivery is another factor to influence the student who chooses the university to study. Nowadays, university teaching method include face to face, online and hybrid modes of course delivery. However, the several ways to students to deliver their coursework, such as full time, part time, internal/ on campus, external studies/distance education, "summer school, winter school, semester study and trimester study." The multi site of a university, e.g. major popular provider of distance online education operates a flexible learning for student to use internet to study. It can reduce face to face contact between teachers and students into university classrooms. Although, it is a technological and innovative and effective learning modalities. In fact, such new technological teaching modalities may be necessitated to the graduated students or master degree or doctoral degree students. But, I feel the online teaching method is not suitable to the bachelor degree students. As the delivery of course content or the commoditization of knowledge must be re-thought to the bachelor degree students because whose knowledge level is limited if the student can't ask whose lecturer any questions by face to face contact. So, students will feel difficult to learn if who can't listen whose lecturers' teaching and to enquire any questions and to give feedback in classrooms immediately. It is possible that who will wait long time to ask many questions to prepare to wait lecturers to give feedback by email later if their lecturers use online teaching method. So it is essential that educators and administrators need to understand differentiated teaching demand to different knowledge level of students. Because student preferences may vary by age, cultural, background, degree types, learning style and matter etc. factors to decide whether whose students are suitable to teach by either online distance learning method between individual student and whose computer or face to face learning method between students and the lecturer in classroom face to face oral teaching educational method. In fact, working adults remain strongly associated eith interest in online delivery. However, the availability of evening/weekend choices is the second most important enrollment factor to adult students, due to who consider when enrolling in an institution to indicate the important of face-to-face traditional delivery at not convenient times. So, online education is most clearly suited to independent learners those individuals who are self-motivated and self reliant and those who have a problem solving orientation.

The 2006 year Eduventures survey found that students interested in associate, bachelor's and master's degrees were most open to whole online delivery, although who were also open to campus-based delivery. Similarly, Gartner's 2008 year e-learning survey found that complete graduate programs offered online continue online. For example, international student demand for Australian higher education is expected to exceed supply in 2020 year, and key 2025 year there will be a shortfall of 22,692 international places on projected demand of 290,848. There numbers imply that to meet demand, Australian universities may want to invest further in online degree/delivery options. However, recent statistics indicate dealing interest in fully online programs in South East Asia, and a survey of 469 transnational students in 2007 year found that a majority of students opposed online provision. These findings suggest that, when branch campuses are found to be prohibitively expensive, the future of transnational programs is in programs that include face-to-face interaction facilitated by an offshore partner of the educational provider. However, education consumers prefer to combine online delivery and geographical proximity. Some of students who are living close to university campus. So who can access to courses delivered in a traditional mode, but chose to take online courses for the flexibility to it afforded them. This is an increasing trend in U.S. institutions as well, whereas online courses are used to cater solely to non-traditional students at a long distance from the campus, increasingly such classes are made available to the mainstream student constituency.

Whetheronline and hybrid courses will influence to university students to choose the university to study.

How can the technology online teaching contributing improve student outcome? At least, learning outcomes for students in online and hybrid courses match those of students in traditional settings. When these are reasons to believe that the hybrid model would produce more effective learning outcomes than the fully-online model in theory. Also evidence suggests that e-learning continues to grow in popularity with the number of hybrid or blended courses increasing at the fastest rate, although online/ hybrid courses certainly do not outcomes courses presented the traditional (i.e. face-to-face traditional classroom) delivery method. These facts help to demonstrate that despite the popularity and increased availability of online courses. However, students still value traditional classroom methods and that online options may not significantly detract from on-campus enrollments.

Hybrid degree programs, also known as blended programs are courses of study that combine traditional classroom based instruction with significant amounts of online instruction, with each passing semester, hybrid degree programs become increasingly popular for students and universities alike. Such courses allow students to reduce time-consuming trips to campus when still benefiting from face-to-face teaching method allow colleges and universities to more effectively use classroom space and to reduce cost. For these reasons, hybrid courses are often praised as the best of both classroom and online teaching methods, it is possible that students have chance to go to classroom to listen lecturer's teaching and who also have chance to use internet to learn from online teaching method as the same time. These is no standard model for hybrid education. Some programs may have students split their time evenly between online and on-campus instruction; some may have students complete the majority of their work online with occasional intensive weekends of on-campus activity and some require students to enroll in a combination of traditional classes as well as strictly online classes. Nowadays, a major educational consulting group found that hybrid or blended learning was the most rapidly growing delivery option when online, hybrid and traditional delivery options were taken into account. Because of the trend towards more hybrid programming, university officials concern on their potential impact on enrollment levels for on-campus degree programs. Some speculate that hybrid programs have the potential to overtake traditional programs, when others hope to use hybrid programs as stepping stones to attract more students to campus on a full time basis. The structures of different programs reflect institutions' intent to use hybrid programs to attract students from non-traditional areas. For example, Michigam State university's Master of social work hybrid program accepts roughly 25 students per year. In 2008 year, these students lived anywhere from 85 to 435 miles from the main campus, therefore frequent in person activities were not feasible. Gather in addition to completing online assignments, students attended a one-week-summer institute on campus in June and face-to-face instruction sessions in smaller groups organized by geography once per month during the fall and spring semesters. In short, hybrid programs do not necessarily replace on-campus offerings, nor do they commonly draw more students to campus on a full time basis. Rather, they complement existing program offerings by reaching out to new packets of students who have the mean to visit campus on occasion but not regularly.

In conclusion, any university ought follow its subjects, student age, school location and tuition, lecturers' reputation and school research facilities etc. factors to decide whether the course is suitable to be chose either online teaching or face-to-face traditional classroom teaching or hybrid (online and face-to-face both) teaching method to teach whose different degree level students. Because these factors will influence who to choose which kind of subjects to study. For example, if many first year students feel the subjects are difficult to learn. It implies that online distance teaching or hybrid teaching method is not suitable to be taught to them. The traditional face-to-face contact traditional classroom teaching method is more suitable to be taught to them. So, it is flexible to any one of these teaching method to choose to teach any subjects to university student. It is no absolute suitable teaching method to teach any one of subject in any one of university. Because any university is independent, it means that the teaching method is suitable to be taught to the students in the university. It doesn't mean that the same teaching method is suitable to be taught to the students to another university because every university's lecturer's reputation, school tuition fee, course's contents and qualities and student age segment and location is different among of them. It is very difficult to ensure which kind of teaching method must be suitable to be taught to the subject to all universities in any countries. Thus, if the university can predict which student individual psychology needs, then it can reduce its student turnover number successfully.

In conclusion, in behavioral economy view point, consumer decision making has long been of interest to research. Such as this university student choice factor, e.g. university location, course design etc. factors can influence students to choose which university to study. The most prevalent model from this perspective is " utility theory" which proposes that consumers make choices based on the expected outcomes of their decisions. Some consumption psychologists view consumers are as rational decision makers and who are only concerned with self interest. However, utility theory views the consumer as a rational economic man. Consumer behavior considers a wide range of factors how to influence to change the consumer behavior , and acknowledges a board range of consumption activities beyond purchasing.

These activities commonly include need recognition, information search, evaluation of alternatives, the building of purchasing intention, the act of purchasing, consumption and final disposal. Some psychologists regard man and rational and self interested, making decisions based upon the ability to maximize utility when spending the minimum effort.

It concerns economic man theory, in order to behavior rationally in the economic sense, as consumers must aware of all the available consumption options be capable of correctly rating each alternative and be available to select the optimum course of action. Some psychologists view point, behavior is subject to biological influence through instinctive force or drives with act outside of conscious thought. So, the consumption psychological behavior is determined by biological drives, rather than individual cognition, or environmental stimuli thoughts and feelings can be regarded as consumer behaviors.

Some psychologists feel environmental variables influence consumer behaviors. However, an influential role of the environment and social experience is acknowledged with consumers activity seeking and receiving environmental and stimuli is as informational inputs aiding internal decision making . Input variables are the environmental stimuli that consumer is subjected to influence to choose either to buy or not buy the product, e.g. brand, advertisement, price, sale channel, place, salespeople service, quality, loyalty, durability etc. different elements can influence consumer final decision making.

Some investigations indicated about the changes in consumer behavior are caused by external environment influences, e.g. globalization and development of information technologies. It can help to understand the specific factors what should be taken into account in evaluation of consumer behavior.

In macroeconomic environment view point, for example, the global trend of economic liberalization, new political geography, gradual removal of international trade barriers , rapid technological advancement these environmental factors are just a few of the factors that have had major effect on the business management practices nowadays. The most obvious impact on the practical level of doing business has these macroeconomic environmental factors intensified competition. So, these factors can influence micro economical consumer behavior indirectly. Consumer behavior is mix of elements from psychology, sociology, sociopsychology, anthropology and economic. Management process will identifies, anticipates and supplies customer requirement efficiently and profitably.

In consumption psychological view point, technical criteria concerns the cost aspects of purchase, durability, reliability, comfort and convenience. Economic criteria concerns the cost aspects of purchase, include price, running costs and residual values, e.g. a trade in value of a car.

In conclusion, economic environmental and consumption psychological factors can influence consumer behavior changing, so businessmen can attempt to do any surveys, experiment etc. research methods to predict how consumer behavior will change to attract them to choose to buy their products more easily.

V

Influencing traveler times psychology factor

For airline industry, if the airline firm can predict global economy trend how to influence oil or gas price, then it can predict its passenger consumption of choice more easily. Due to we are entering globalization. In Special, airline transportation demands are also increasing, due to many travelers need to catch planes to travel as well as many cargoes need to be carried to planes to transport to different countries to sell. It seems aviation transportation industry is important to influence the health of the global economy growth nowadays. However, ignorance of internal or external market dynamics, catching travelers business can be detrimental to airline profitability more than carrying cargoes business. Because the demands of travelling different countries‘ travelers’ consumption are still more than the demands of businessmen carrying cargoes in any countries every year. So, the passenger income sector is still have the important position to compare to cargo income sector in global airline transportation industry any countries nowadays.

How can negative social change influence any airlines' air ticket prices to be risen to influence cost raising? In fact, the increase in petroleum price can have chance to affect airlines in a negative manner because increased oil prices have resulted in the reduction of services operations, the number of airline schedules flights, even airline bankruptcies. Whether inflation, terrorism, oil price, bank interest rate etc. external factors have the most influential to cause the bad effects to cause airlines need to raise air ticket price to influence traveler numbers to be decreased.

To support this hypotheses, these are my research questions, such as : Does a combination of terrorism and price of petroleum significantly influence airline profit changing mostly? The alternative hypothesis was whether a significant relationship exists between terrorism, price of petroleum and airline profitability more than other factors, such as inflation, bank interest rate of these factors cause to ticket price raising. I shall indicate that the first assumption was that terrorism has a negative effect on airline profitability and another assumption was that only external factors as oil prices or terrorism affect airline profitability.

What is the relationship of oil price and terrorism to airline industry to influence ticket price increasing ?

However the effects of oil price and terrorism on airline profitability was limited to a regional perspective, e.g. the terrorism attack of plane crash event to USA on 11 Sept. After the terrorism attack happened on USA 11 Sept. incident of terrorism attack was restricted to events of skyjacking, attacks on oil production, refinery and distribution. Other types of terrorist activities, such as attacks on financial targets or senior government officials could have an adverse effect on the petroleum and airline industry. I think the disruption of the production or distribution of petroleum because of incidents of terrorism was costly in terms of loss of business and the inflationary effect on fuel dependent products or services.

In fact, some airlines have adopted more fuel saving technology, so whose fuel consumption would not use more than other non fuel saving technology airlines, these own fuel saving technology airlines which do not need to increase ticket prices to influence passenger numbers to be decreased in possible. It seems fuel price increasing will not be the only factor to influence the airline industry's traveler numbers decreasing, in addition to terrorism external incident factor influence. However, due to some airlines which have fuel saving technology, so which can avoid to use more fuel to provide planes to use and which fuel costs will be reduced, then which can provide cheaper air ticket fare prices to compare the non fuel saving technology airlines. The result will cause some airlines will lose travelling customers in this global airline travelling market, also the non fuel saving technology airlines need to renew their fuel technology if which want to keep their competitive abilities to avoid to close down their businesses.

Also, I shall indicate the financial risk of airline industry evidence from Cathay Pacific airways and China airlines against key determinants of which include interest rate, exchange rate and fuel price risk for the period of January 1996 year to December 2011 year. During this period, these key external factors which were the most serious influence to cause these two airlines choose to change their strategic behaviors. Due to any these financial risks is difficult to predict and it was also changing often, these factors will also affect any airlines stock returns which arise from changing economic conditions, e.g. fuel price movements and fluctuations in exchange rates. These external unpredicted changing factors will attribute to the air tickets cyclical demand, capital investment, fixed costs of labor and landing rights to this global airline industry.

However, the relationship between fuel price and stock prices varies across economies. The effects of oil price changes in sub-sector indices, such as wood, paper and printing, insurance and electricity. In the past, on global stock exchange market was positively significant in 2011 year. Otherwise, with respect to the U.S.A. aviation industry, some economists suggested that global airlines stock returns were negatively to percentage change in fuel prices related to any airline firm value, e.g. Qantas and Air New Zealand were negatively share price growth to fuel price risk in the short term in the 2011 year. Thus, airline industry needs to concern whether the effects of oil price changes in sub-sector indices, such as wood, paper and printing, insurance and electricity influences to predict when oil price will increase or decrease because it will lead to influence its passenger travelling numbers indirectly and these sub-sector industries have close relationship to bring cause and effect influence to oil price to airline industry.

VI

Influence passenger catching underground train psychology factor

How does MTR (Mass Train Railway) need to consider route design location of choice

Nowadays, transportation and economic development have close relationship. Economic development stimulates transportation demand by increasing the numbers of workers commuting to and from work, customers traveling to and from services areas, and products being moving by lorries on the roads between products and customers. According to Bailey, Mokhtarian and Little (2008) indicated "transportation route is past of distinct development pattern or road network and mostly described by regular street patterns as an important factor of human existence, development and civilization. The route network combined with increased road transportation investment result in changed levels of conveniently reflected through cost benefit analysis, savings in travel time, and other benefits. " These benefits are noticeable in increased catchment areas for services and facilities , shops, schools, offices, banks and leisure activities by transportation route design of location choice.

Why MTR underground train transportation needs to know passenger behavior

Understanding individual passenger behavior is essential for the design MTR transportation, because who can choose to catch bus, taxi, tram, train ferry etc. different kinds of public transportation tools. Individual traveler who decides to catch which kinds of public transportation tools, it depends on whether the public transportation tool can provide real time travel information, liking link travel time schedule. So, any country's (MTR) mass transit railway transportation enterprises need to understand where it has terminal to give convenience to the local living areas of time travelers to choose to catch MTR easily. Although, MTR ticket fare is one factor to influence any passengers choice. But, those other factors can also influence them to choice. e.g. MTR any terminal location of convenience, short time travelling, none crowding in busy (peak) time, MTR platform waiting arrival time, none sudden MTR engineering machines broken accident events occurrence frequently etc. different factors, any one of these factors which can influence passengers who choose to catch MTR or other kinds of transportation tools.

Why route choice can influence passenger behavioral choice ?

Usually, the busy time passengers will regard the route choice as a coordination problem to influence them to choose to catch which kinds of transportation tools. The route choice is as an opportunity costs to influence any busy time passengers to decide to choose to catch which kind of transportation tool which is the best right choice in the right time among of them. In the short time, for example, it seems any busy time passengers will choose to catch bus to substitute MTR underground train transportation tool, due to who feels the bus can arrive any destinations to compare other kinds of transportation tools in the most short time. However even if the MTR can either charge cheaper ticket fare to sell full day or charge discount ticket fare to sell in the busy (peak) time to compare to bus fare. It is possible that the busy time passengers will still choose to catch bus, if between the bus terminal and the another bus terminal that distance is the shorter time route to spend time to arrive destination to compare between the MTR terminal to the another MTR terminal arrival time . Also, although the busy time passengers will feel to encounter traffic jam to influence sitting or waiting bus time to be longer time in possible and who also feel MTR can avoid traffic jam problem. However, usually any busy (peak) time passengers will feel the chance of traffic jam occurrence will be less. So, the short bus route choice is more potential factor to influence the busy (peak) time passengers still to choose bus to catch.

However, if anyone wants to investigate results of day-to-day route choice which can be transferred to more realistic environment. It is necessary to explore individual behavior in an interactive experimental set up to ensure busy (peak) time passenger transportation behavioral choice. For example, a passenger has a choice between a main road (M) and a side road (S) for travelling from (A) to (B). (M) is faster if (M) and (S) are chose by the same number of passengers. So, this method can be researched whether MTR terminal station is located at the main road (M) or the side road (S) where is more suitable to accept to passengers generally.

Why trip time reliability and crowding factors can influence MTR passenger choice ?

Other problem is MTR busy (peak) time's crowding in public transportation occurrence of MTR underground train transportation tool is becoming a growth to concern as MTR demand growth at a busy (peak) time. To capture the MTR passengers benefits with reduced crowding from improved MTR public transport service and image. It is necessary a identify the relevant dimensions of crowding that are meaningful measures of what crowding means to MTR passengers. Two main influences on MTR model choice that are growing in relevance are trip time reliability and crowding. It represents a benefit-cost framework. In fact, MTR passengers can be willing to pay more expensive ticket fare, it MTR can avoid crowding and short and the accurate arrival trip time between terminals is reliable to occur. How to measure of MTR crowding, e.g. weighting the gap between the busy time, the standard (i.e. objective) and the perceived (i.e. subjective) metrics. We are not in a position to definitely map the two dimensions, which is a crucial requirement for translating objective improvements into equivalent subjective gains that then can be applied, willingness to pay estimates MTR ticket fares to obtain the additional MTR passenger benefits of MTR public transportation investment to any terminal stations.

Because MTR crowding has a negative impact on passengers in terms of psychological on emotional distress. MTR passengers are willing to stand for up to 20 minutes of the service is fast and reliable usually. However crowding outweighed these benefits from a MTR passenger's perpective, experienced crowding leads a increased dissatisfaction. e.g. stress and less privacy during who needs to stand up in MTR. Due to there are no enough places to supply to them to stand up in MTR. If the MTR trip time was longer time between the passenger's terminals, who will feel more dissatisfaction and it will cause who feels whether who ought need to choose to catch other transportation tools to substitute MTR next time. e.g. bus, train, tram, ferry, taxi etc. So, from an operator's perspective, the MTR service frequency or

MTR size is significantly influenced by the level of ridership, which sends a signal to respond if the monitored crowding level exceeds the benchmark standard in the busy time. e.g. in the morning time or at the night time, the students or employment people who need to go to schools or offices (working places). The locations of different places between MTR terminals and crowding are regarded as a key service attribute for MTR pubic transportation along with other factors, such as travelling time and reliability, e.g. service quality, none engineering machines are broken to cause MTR stops suddenly.

Given the increasing importance of crowding on both the disutility to existing MTR public transportation users and the influence to it. MTR passenger can choose to use either the MTR public transportation or other public transportation. It is timely to review the MTR current measures of crowding defined by transportation authorities. MTR operators ought evaluate whether they appropriately reflect MTR each traveler experiences and perceptions of crowding in busy (peak) time. I suggest that MTR needs to buy other underground trains to supply to the busy (peak) time passengers to let them have enough seats to sit down, so who do not need to stand up in any MTR underground trains when they catch MTR underground trains in busy time. It aims to let who are willingness to pay the estimation of reasonable ticket fares to compare the other kinds of transportation tools in the busy (peak) time.

How MTR can attract many passengers by survey method?

On the commuter departure time choice of any reference point researching hand, the departure time decisions of communters are of fundamental importance of peak period MTR traffic congestion. However, whether on the demand side, MTR underground train congestion relief measures, such as MTR ticket fare to every terminal station needs to be charged cheaper fare or discount fare in the peak (busy) time every day. To aim to attract many passengers to choose to catch MTR Underground train public transportation tools, substitute to choose other public transportation tools in the peak time.

Over the past decades, there have been very active research efforts in the departure time problem, both in econometric modeling and dynamic user equilibrium fields. Although, these works provide valuable insights into dynamic commuter decision making, they do not identify the commuters' response to gains and losses related to whole actual arrival time to reference points who may have relative. The applicability of the reference point hypothesis of prospect theory to the commuter's departure time decision making to obtain a better understanding of how departure time choice in MTR platform during their waiting underground train arrival time. However, every MTR underground train actual arrival time and deviation variables related to reference points (gains and losses) are the key factors in the departure time choice model. How the MTR underground train of every communter's daily departure time decision can be modelled when the reference point hypothesis of prospect theory. The MTR underground train's schedule delay is defined as the difference between the preferred arrival time (PAT) and the actual arrival time (AT) for a given MTR communter. In a daily MTR commute, a commuter in the indifference band actual arrival time is an essential feature of MTR schedule study. Two reference points are the earliest acceptable arrival time and the work starting time for a given MTR platform waiting passengers. In psychological view point, prospect theory proposes that the displeasure of a loss is perceived or greater than the pleasure of a gain of the same attitude and therefore, the value function is stronger for losses than gains.

To conclude, it seems that if MTR waiting passengers need not spend long time to wait underground train arrival in platform and it can provide seats to let them to sit down in the busy (peak) crowding time. It will make them to feel pleasure, even the MTR ticket fare is not fair and reasonable to charge higher fare to compare other kinds of public transportation tools fares. So the peak waiting time factor can influence the passengers to choose other kind of transportation tools to catch easily. Moreover, MTR's two reference points are the earliest role. Similarly a loss is observed when the MTR platform waiting commuter experiences or actual arrival time which is beyond that the MTR schedule time. Due to that a MTR waiting commuter is as an early side arrival of whose actual arrival time is earlier than whose preferred arrival time.

In general, passenger transportation choice consumption behavior is similar to alcohol choice consumption behavior. Because some passengers choose to catch the kind of transportation tool , it is habit cause. Such as some alcohol consumers who often drive the brand of alcohol , it is habit cause also.

Some consumption psychologists had attempt to research whether planned behavior can predict alcohol consumption. This research aims to quantify variables between theory of planned behavior variables and (i) intentions to consume alcohol in habit and (ii) reducing alcohol consumption reasons. They showed some drunken violence alcohol consumers who will reduce to consume much alcohol if who feel driving accident or causing death or violence behavior or alcohol poison causing non-health after who have consumed too much alcohol often. Thus, it is important to understand the psychological determinants of alcohol consumption.

A model of human behavior that has been extensively utilized to predict health-related behaviors, such as alcohol consumption in the theory planned (TPB; Ajzen, 1991). This model proposes that the most important determinant of behavior is a person's intention to perform the behavior. Three variables are identified as determinants intention, attitude, subjective norm and perceived behavioral control . Attitudes are an individual's positive or negative evaluation of performing the behavior. Subjective norms reflect an individual's perceptions of social approach or disapproval for performing the behavior. It represents an individual's perceptions of control over behavioral performance in the face of internal and external barriers. These results suggest the possibility that alcohol consumer behavior that are harmful to health, such as alcohol consumption, may yield different relationships when compared with results for behaviors that are beneficial to health. Specifically, individuals may wish to emphasis a lack of control over health risk behaviors, because these behaviors are not seen as socially , desirable and may need to be explained away be reference to external causes, such as peer pressure (De Visser & Mc Donnell, 2013).

It seems that the passenger will reduce times to catch the kind of transportation tool if who feels the kind of transportation is dangerous (not safe) , such as if the alcohol consumer feels the alcohol will cause not health to him/her. Then, who will also reduce times to choose to buy the brand of alcohol to drink.

Hence, it seems fear feeling psychological factor can influencealcohol consumers to reduce alcohol consumption in these situations, such as what action is being considered (e.g. heavy episodic drinking and the action is located (e.g. driving car) and what is the time frame for the action(e.g. needs car), the staff is a company driver when needs to drive car every day. Thus, whose action will influence to reduce whose alcohol consumption. Although, who has drinking alcohol in habit, but because who is one company driver, who is fear to cause accident to hurt himself/herself and whose staffs when who sit in whose company car together. So, who will choose to reduce to consume alcohol in possible. Hence, dangerous is one most factor to influence passengers who do not choose to catch it.

However, social mobile analysis is a good method to research what the main factors which can influence passengers to either choose to catch MTR or choose other transportation tools, such as bus, tram, train, ferry , taxi etc. Some consumption psychologists had using a data set involving on adults (26 couples) living in a community for over a year to find that social behavior measured via face-to-face interaction, call and SMS logs, which can be used to predict the spending behavior to explore diverse business because loyal customers and overspend. Their results showed the mobile phone bases social interaction patterns can provide more predictive power on spending behavior than personality based features. Interestingly , these consumption psychologists found that more social couples also tend to overspend. Obtaining such insights about couple level spending behavior via novel social-computing frameworks can be of vital importance to economists, marketing professional and policy markers.

The basic idea is that a person's attitudes and behaviors are influenced by several levels of society, such as culture, subculture, social classes, reference groups and face-to-face groups. Such as any passenger's transportation tools choice, which are also influenced by culture, subculture, social classes, near transportation tool place, transportation cost, transportation time schedule and transportation service etc. factors.

In Special finally, some consumption psychologists investigated whether the social behavior measured via face-to-face interactions, call and SMS logs can be used to predict the spending behavior for couples in terms of their propensity to explore diverse businesses, engage frequently with them and overspend. Their findings not only motivate in potentially new line of investigation into a spending behavior via mobile sensing , but also demonstrate the feasibility of passive (i.e. which don't require active user attention) method, for undertaking similar studies at a large scale in near future.

In recent years, mobile sensing and reality approaches have been used to understand multiple aspects of human behavior. Insights on a behavioral level (e.g. overspending, loyalty and diversity) have much longer term validity and can explain certain aspects of human behavior. To study spending behavior of couples, the consumption psychologists focus on three important behavior : exploration, loyalty and overspending behavior. The aim is to identify the couples that tend to explore diverse business, engages repeatedly and frequently with certain businesses and (or) spend higher amounts of income to them. For exploration, who calculated the diversity in vendors frequented. The exact method for calculating diversity scores is explained in the next section. For loyalty, who considered how frequently couples engage with their favorite businesses. Specifically, they calculated the percentage of transactions (out of a couple's total transactions), that were made at their top businesses. Lastly, to quantify overspending, they calculated the ratio of the amount of money spent by a couple to their self-declared discretionary spending budget. Hence MTR can use mobile to enquire what are the general expectation to any passengers in order to predict the reasons why who prefer to choose other transporation tools more accurate.

How to apply online psychological advertising method to predict passenger behavioral consumption?

Online advertising can give relevance information to represent the similarity between advertisement and queries. These existing online advertisement works mainly focused on interpreting advertisements clicks in term of what consumers seek. (i.e. relevance information) and how consumers choose to watch TV or magazine or online advertisement etc. from different promotion media. (historically to know the product is selling on the market through advertising information). However, few of manufacturers or sellers attempted to understand why consumers chose to watch the advertising from TV or magazine or internet etc. different media.

Why can MTR can choose online advertisement to predict passenger behavior? Online Advertisement can be as a commercial search engine for manufacturers or sellers to gather data to concern how behavioral consumption is. The online advertisement's each observations motivate who to systemically model to test what each consumer individual psychological desire in order for a precise prediction on behavioral consumption after online advertisement promotion from internet media.

Today, internet is one kind of effective psychological advertising promotion method. For example, an online advertisement system, sponsored search has been one of the most important business models for commercial web search engines. It generates most of the revenue of search engines by presenting to users sponsored search results, i.e. advertisements (ads), along with organic search results. To deliver the most interesting ads to the users, a sponsored search system consists of technical components, including query-to-ads matching, online click prediction for matched ads, online click probability and auction to determine the ranking, placement, and pricing of the remaining ads. To aim to attempt to predict behavioral consumption for any kinds of product sale from online advertisement media.

In today's industry, generalized second price auction (GSP) is the most widely-used auction mechanism , in which the price that an advertiser has to pay depends on the predicted online click probability of the online buyers, whose own ads as well as the bid price and predicted online click probability of the ads ranked in the next position. The online sponsored search systems typically employ a machine learning model top predict the probability that an online user clicks an advertising from internet.

However, in practical sponsored search system. There are many ads without adequate historical click through data, even after query levels. Then online ads can been click improved prediction accuracy to consumer individual behavioral consumption when each click is occurred to the seller individual website. For example, online ads, such as : free Nike coupons ad. It shows " Go-Get_couptons.com/Nike, Download and print Nike coupons (100% Free)" ; another Nike-sales prices ad. It shows www.calibex.com, clothing, latest fashions and styles on sale. Buy Nike Fast!" ; another Perfume.com official site ad. It shows "www.perfume.com, 10,000 + brand name perfumes and colognes-up to 80% off retail!" ; another Luxury English Perfume Ad. It shows " www.florislondon.com, shop online for luxury perfumes for men, women and the home". Above of these are example online ads. For two queries, "Nike" and "Perfume" , and two ads under the same query field similar relevance to the query.

Despite the usefulness of the relevance and historical of what users click and how users click. Specially, relevance information can indicate what relevant content users seek to click from online (internet) media. However, as it is well-known that users are not active to search for ads., the search engine, instead has to recommend ads. To users during their generic web search. Therefore, the relevance between query and ad can't perform as the key driver for click. In my opinion, in order for more click prediction, businessmen need to examine why users click.

Thus, MTR can use online advertisement to gather any passenger opinions concerning these questions: What will influence them to choose to catch other transportation tools, instead of MTR? What are MTR passengers expectations when who are catching MTR transportation tool? etc. different consumption psychologial questions.

How to apply psychological research to analyze of online user desire in sponsored search for behavioral consumption of reasons? First, according to literatures on consumer behavioral analyses, many factors will influence the decision making for consumption, including thought based effects and feeling-based effects. Though-based effects are basically win or loss analysis (e.g. trade-off between price and quantity), when feeling-based effects are more subjective (e.g. brand loyalty and luxury seeking). Note users online clicking the ad. Usually are with the intention to purchase something. In this situation, it is natural that the factors mentioned in consumer behavior analyses will influence their online click behaviors.

So, MTR advertisers can gather online advertisement data to choose how to design whose online advertisement to follow either is based on win or loss analysis, either focusing on MTR ticket price and MTR service performance quality features or is based on more subjective analysis , focusing on MTR brand loyalty and luxury(high income passenger segment) seeking features to attract any MTR passengers individual attention to choose to watch MTR online advertisements from online advertisement media more easily. So, it seems that online advertisement is a promotional and gathering data channel to persuade MTR passenger individual attention to predict these influence factor: how to change or improve MTR service performance or MTR station location choice or how to arrange busy time and non busy time MTR ticket price etc. influence factor in order to design MTR online advertisement to attract many passengers change their attitude to prefer choose to catch MTR transportation tools.

9 798887 726205

Printed by Libri Plureos GmbH in Hamburg, Germany